The Arranged Marriage

MARY BURRITT CHRISTIANSEN POETRY SERIES
Hilda Raz, Series Editor

The Mary Burritt Christiansen Poetry Series publishes two to four books a year that engage and give voice to the realities of living, working, and experiencing the West and the Border as places and as metaphors. The purpose of the series is to expand access to, and the audience for, quality poetry, both single volumes and anthologies, that can be used for general reading as well as in classrooms.

Mary Burritt
Christiansen
Poetry Series

Also available in the Mary Burritt Christiansen Poetry Series:

Report to the Department of the Interior: Poems by Diane Glancy
The Sky Is Shooting Blue Arrows: Poems by Glenna Luschei
A Selected History of Her Heart: Poems by Carole Simmons Oles
The Goldilocks Zone by Kate Gale
Flirt by Noah Blaustein
Progress on the Subject of Immensity by Leslie Ullman
Losing the Ring in the River by Marge Saiser
Say That by Felecia Caton Garcia
City of Slow Dissolve by John Chávez
Breaths by Eleuterio Santiago-Díaz

For additional titles in the Mary Burritt Christiansen Poetry Series, please visit unmpress.com.

The Arranged Marriage

poems

JEHANNE DUBROW

UNIVERSITY OF NEW MEXICO PRESS • ALBUQUERQUE

Library of Congress Cataloging-in-Publication Data
Dubrow, Jehanne.
 [Poems. Selections]
 The arranged marriage : poems / Jehanne Dubrow.
     pages cm. — (Mary Burritt Christiansen poetry series)
 ISBN 978-0-8263-5553-9 (pbk. : alk. paper) — ISBN 978-0-8263-5554-6 (electronic)
 I. Title.
 PS3604.U276A6 2015
 811'.6—dc23
                              2014015417

Cover photograph courtesy of Kristina Smith
Author photograph courtesy of Cedric Terrell
Book design by Catherine Leonardo
Composed in Helvetica Std Roman
Display type is SchmutzICG Clogged

Contents

Acknowledgments   vii

The Handbag   1
A Grounding for the Metaphysics of Morals   2
Makeshift Bandage   3
Malamute   4
Her Right Ankle   5
Rules for Passover in the Tropics   6
All the Sharp Things   7
Tourist Trap   8
Bespoke   9
Bruise in the Shape of a Hand   10
My Mother, Age Five, Dressed as Mata Hari   11
Scheherazade   12
Arranged Marriage, as Coffee Field   13
Portrait of My Mother's Father, with Peppercorns and Vinegar   14
Milagro Umbrella Factory   15
Mother-in-Law   16
House of the Small Dictatorship   17
The Epileptic   18
The Woman in the Grocery Store   19
Still Life   20
Hostage   21
Domesticated Fowl of the Sula Valley   22
My Mother Wonders—   23
Lapdog   24
Shot through with Holes   25

In Honduras, My Grandmother Dreamed of Germany   26

Interview   27

Story   28

Dubrovnik   29

Lost Photograph of Trotsky, from the Family Album   30

Portrait of My Mother's First Husband, with Fabergé Objects   31

The Blue Dress   32

Ode to Breaking Things   33

Doubt   35

Eros and Psyche   36

Willful Abandonment   37

Tower   38

Limen   39

My Mother, Temporarily Disowned   40

Chronic Pain   41

When Her Father Was Losing at Poker, Her Mother Said   42

Café con leche   43

The Replacement Ring   44

Set Jerusalem above My Highest Joy   45

My Mother Hurts Her Hand Again   46

Bethesda   47

The Leap   48

What I Saw in the Water; Or, What the Water Gave Me   49

Family Business   50

Garment Industry   51

Strawberry Thief   52

Met Parents My How   53

Schiller   54

Light Switch   55

Notes   57

Acknowledgments

AGNI Online: "Eros and Psyche"

Bellevue Literary Review: "Bruise in the Shape of a Hand" and "Interview"

Birmingham Poetry Review: "Milagro Umbrella Factory" and "Lost Photograph of Trotsky, from the Family Album"

Black Warrior Review: "Malamute"

Bosque: "Domesticated Fowl of the Sula Valley"

Boulevard: "House of the Small Dictatorship"

Cincinnati Review: "Doubt" and "Light Switch"

Copper Nickel: "All the Sharp Things," "Chronic Pain," "A Grounding for the Metaphysics of Morals," and "The Handbag"

Crazyhorse: "The Leap" and "Shot through with Holes"

Diode: "Café con leche," "The Replacement Ring," and "Set Jerusalem above My Highest Joy"

Epiphany: "Dubrovnik" and "Tower"

Gulf Coast: "Still Life"

Memorious: "Scheherazade"

Meridian: "Portrait of My Mother's Father, with Peppercorns and Vinegar" and "Family Business"

New Orleans Review: "Bespoke," "Tourist Trap," and "What I Saw in the Water; Or, What the Water Gave Me"

Ninth Letter: "Arranged Marriage, as Coffee Field"

Plume: "The Epileptic"

Prairie Schooner: "Strawberry Thief"

Southern Review: "Bethesda," "Makeshift Bandage," and "Schiller"

Third Coast: "Her Right Ankle" and "Story"

Verse Daily: "Malamute"

Water~Stone Review: "Hostage"

West Branch: "Mother-in-Law"
Zeek: "Rules for Passover in the Tropics"

❧

"A Grounding for the Metaphysics of Morals" and "Schiller" were included in *Women Write Resistance: Poets Resist Gender Violence* edited by Laura Madeline Wiseman (Hyacinth Girl Press, 2013).

❧

A group of poems from the book were selected by Claudia Rankine to receive the 2012 Alice Fay Di Castagnola Award from the Poetry Society of America.

❧

"Rules for Passover in the Tropics" was one of a group of poems awarded first place in the 2011 Anna Davidson Rosenberg Poetry Award for Poems on the Jewish Experience.

❧

"Limen" (under the title "Poem on the Dedication of the Hillel House, at Washington College, on Maryland's Eastern Shore") was printed as a limited-edition broadside by the Literary House Press at the Rose O'Neill Literary House.

❧

My gratitude to those who encouraged me—in small ways and large—at moments when I was most uncertain: Tarfia Faizullah, Meredith Davies Hadaway, Leslie Harrison, James Magruder, Mathias Svalina, and to Erika Meitner, who helped *The Arranged Marriage* find its final shape. My great thanks to Hilda Raz—dear teacher, mentor, and editor of the Mary Burritt Christiansen Poetry Series. And thank you to Elise McHugh, senior acquisitions editor at University of New Mexico Press, for giving this book such a good home.

My love and thanks to my father, Stephen, and my brother, Eric.

Jeremy, you continue to be the best DoctorPoetHusband ever. I love you in the whole wide world. Argos, my puppy pasha, you kept me safe and protected during the writing of this collection; I miss your fuzzy presence every day.

And to my mother, Jeannette, who let me borrow her story for a little while. *Thank you* for these poems.

The Arranged Marriage

The Handbag

From the back of the closet, where old coats are rubbing shoulders—wool on wool, and felt on felt—my mother pulls the purse she never uses, heavy bottomed one, four metal feet that scrape, inside deep enough to confine a bowling ball. What the man doesn't know is that the bag is full of borrowed books rigid at their spines. The man with the knife. What the man doesn't know: in the left pocket, a compact still holding its cracked mirror. Ballpoint pen. Lipstick in a shade of pink like someone being pinched. So when my mother drops the shopping list into the open mouth of her handbag, clicking shut magnetic snaps, the man is thinking of the food he'll eat tonight. Spaghetti. Meatballs. This meal she'll cook for him. And my mother is thinking about the store a few blocks from here, the one facing a street of strangers. And the police station. She's testing the heft of leather handles, weighing the spring-loaded frame of this thing, wondering how hard she'll have to swing.

A Grounding for the Metaphysics of Morals

Or perhaps the story starts with books on her table. When the man breaks in, she's sleeping. Tomorrow: an exam. Tomorrow: a paper due. She's half-asleep, the sound of someone in the room soft as turning pages. First, he tells her, I heard a noise. By he is meant the handyman. And when there is no noise to hear, he bolts the door. He grinds her face into the wood. A cardboard box kicked. A hand bitten. That he will kill her if the night stays gray too long, a kind of a priori knowledge. He read Kant in prison, comics too black and white, dime-store pulp too literal in its black and blue. There is an argument for anything, he says: to drown the small brown dog, to swipe the wallet, even to unlock the girl's apartment where she is falling in her sleep.

Makeshift Bandage

The attacker is bleeding where she bit him. So
she ties a towel to his hand. Times like these,
there should be a kit for cleaning up the mess:
some kind of pill to pulverize, a horn that mouths
a word like STOP. The towel won't stay. She
finds electric tape inside a kitchen drawer. The
tearing sound it makes—nothing should tear
the way a loop of tape uncircles from itself. His
palm, now terrycloth and stickyblack, ripped at
the edges.

Malamute

Someone brought winter to the tropics. At first, it slept near the roots of a strangler tree, curled under chairs, licked salt from sweating ankles. It was content. Table scraps fed its belly. Breezes carried the blue memory of ice. Its teeth were beautiful in the way of sharpened things. Winter tried not to pant. But the little girl kept touching it, kept stroking the curved blade of its tail. Her hands were wet with breakfast. Winter leaped from the dirt, fast as a change in weather. Later, someone would tell the story— how it bit her throat, how bristling and alone it must have been, this December abandoned to the wrong latitude.

Her Right Ankle

is bruised from the hammer he holds in his dominant hand—is turning the dark of her room—is soft where bone should be a hardened thing—and if it made a sound would squish like soggy cloth wrung out—is the pulse of pain she reads about—in poetry—in the history of girls—is the sourness of pills and nothing in the paper cup to wash them down—is cold and hot as hospital sheets—is a smell of burning—is electroshock—is the man with the hammer—is all his padded cells and prison cells—his scribbles on a scrap of envelope—is the hurt he leaves when he comes knocking

Rules for Passover in the Tropics

Your matzoh won't arrive. Convene a kaffeeklatsch. Debate the leavening of corn when mashed to meal. Wine will break in transit. Invent a substitute for the crate of shards and purple stains. Forget apples. Forget there ever was a fruit called apple in the world. Bone is easy to acquire: from the chicken's neck or goat behind the lean-to. No shortage of water mixed with salt. And bitter herb grows wild in these larger valleys. Expect Elijah. Expect Elijah never shows. Tell stories of the mango tree, the tin-roof tines of rain on the tiny synagogue. Name tribes of birds that settle where you stay. Yellow-naped. White-throated. Brown. Olive. And last, because you're faithful to the narrative, hide from the angel of this place, a slice of red above an open door.

All the Sharp Things

First the obvious, the paring knives, the set of steak knives in their burnished box, the long serrated knife for slicing bread, the stubby one not good for anything but butter. And after that, he finds her snub-nosed pliers, her Phillips-head. Even the sewing scissors left open near a spool of thread. Even the porcupine of a pincushion. And other things that never seemed as shrill before—he lays them out, each one a gift she cannot touch, so close the colored pencils, keys, tweezers from the lighted vanity. Wait long enough and anything takes on a sheen of sharpness. Mustn't leave her hands untied. She could stare the whorl from fingertips. Cut him with her eyes.

Tourist Trap

She enters the marriage, as if through a terminal, misplacing her name the way a traveler misplaces a glove. She loses the edges of herself. In his country, she is a tourist who stares at Mayan pyramids. He pleats the map into an easy square, plots a north of his choosing—everything fits flatly in his hands. He rolls the window down, points to ruins on the left. There are fields of indigo, more pink than blue, a worker stooped among the stalks. Trees a thousand years old. Cities hidden beneath volcanic ash. They seldom stop for a longer look, green ruins crowding the side-view mirror, all that collapse much closer than it may appear.

Bespoke

My mother's first marriage was a custom-made suit. It fit expensively. Wool, it scratched her skin, smelled like stale cigar and men playing poker. Her husband tasted of single-malt scotch. What she saw in him was a waltz, a little step, what they called pasillo in those parts, or a tune about the bitterness of love. She wore pearls to her wedding, sure sign of tears, and after was busy as a cockroach in an empty kitchen. When she baked, he kissed jam from her fingers, powdered her with sugar. Bésame, bésame mucho. The stiff fabric of this thing refused to breathe. At night she flew to America and returned each morning to the tiled room. If she stayed in this country, my mother would become the new song of revolution, murder or be murdered. Her window warned of it, her door. Her closet filled with a rack of tailored bodies, each one unmoving, hanging there.

Bruise in the Shape of a Hand

Her face, like one of those ancient caves
where a man has left his signature. Handprint
to say, I was here—this body made of stone
belongs to me. My mother is made of stone.
Before she steps outside, the man demands
foundation the color of skin. Cover yourself, he
says. His palm is everywhere, the little spots
of swelling on her cheek, the wince and squint
of it. How to hide the purple by the eye? The
cut with powder? How to pencil in a pair of
uncontusioned lips?

My Mother, Age Five, Dressed as Mata Hari

Some devil has turned her double agent. She's dancer of the seven veils, high priestess of the cha-cha-cha. Come hither, says the camera. Come kiss me, says the girl. And never mind the questions—who linked the silver chain around her waist? who cuffed her arm? who shot the photograph? Call her bohemian. Call her the kind of trouble that tastes like chocolate, so sweet it doesn't matter what she stains. Call her a danger sharpest to herself. A femme fatale. A firing squad. She's bugle beads and red chiffon, unraveling. Costume makes a courtesan. Costume makes the little mouth a place for poison, for swallowing a string of pearls.

Scheherazade

How can this compare with what I shall tell you this coming night, if I am still alive and the king spares me?
— *One Thousand and One Nights*

Scheherazade must stop the light from entering. Her face: not blood but cut ruby. Her smile: a string of pearls. Tonight she resembles my mother. So like a girl's apartment is her royal chamber, the king like a stranger breaking in. Tell me a story, he says, Tell me why I shouldn't kill you. Shadows of chairs become foreshadowing and the door a frame to frame the tale. Narrative is her neck encircled by his hands. Of proverbs, she has none. Of flowers: the bruised rose, the crushed anemone. Of the king with his fingers on her collarbone, she has this to say: that silk may be used for strangling, that a girl may stab to the silver hilt.

Arranged Marriage, as Coffee Field

1.

The coffee field is not the sugarcane or cotton field: it is a red thing, red-beaded. I used to lose myself, the woman said, but there was a limit to getting lost, where leaves ended and roads began. After she watched the workers strip and pulp, after she breathed the roasted air, dark oils slept in her. The cotton field, like clouds on earth, deceives with so much softness; the coffee field is plainer in its pain. For that year, the field belonged to her, and her body, so shy in its aromas, became almost keen to burn.

2.

The coffee field was never hers, but always his, as was the road that wrapped around. All this is part of me, he used to say, his hands on everything, but there was a border his body ran out and hers began. After he fingered leaves and felt for ripeness, after he sipped the first tastings of the season, he fell asleep. His coffee field, his wife—and what was left but polishing, grading for imperfection in the bean? For that year, she was half-open, waiting to be split or thrown away.

Portrait of My Mother's Father, with Peppercorns and Vinegar

At the perimeter of his property: barrels of salt water. He sank cloves of garlic, rough handfuls of dill. Cucumbers were scored the length of their skins, each fruit striped to let flavor in. Evenings he walked from cask to cask, lifted lids, stirred or tasted the brine with a little finger. He stayed out there past dark, past the point when everything dissolved—the fence, the fig tree, the man thin as switch grass. If you had watched him with the pickles, souring inward toward the seed, that slow fermentation, you would have thought, Here is a patient man. My children, he used to call those green bodies. I'm going to check on my children. When a batch was close to curing, he carried a knife to the yard, tasting the only way to know. He swallowed a slice the shape of a thumb tip. What he wanted was the usual, pleasant pain. And if it was ready, he ate the whole pickle. And if it wasn't, he tossed the cut thing in the bushes.

Milagro Umbrella Factory

The genius of my grandmother was her hands. Once, she unstitched a guy from the machine, his finger a larva pinned to silk. No one else had the nerve to spin the wheel, drive the needle deeper, before raising the shank— although, how else to free his finger? After that, the men began to call her Doña Boss. They watched her break down each engine into rational parts; she worked a screwdriver the size of a pinkie, pinched eyedroppers full of oil. Her office was a wonder of crook handles, tin cups, caps, ribs and stretchers, telescopic tubes. In the beginning, every shade was black. But my grandmother wanted scarab green, purple, the pink of bougainvillea. Parasols for sun, umbrellas for rain. Everything had its proper name. Her columns always added up. This was business that could last as long as weather, because people lose small things in taxicabs. And, of course, another certainty: that it would storm, and someone must build the little roofs.

Mother-in-Law

Conveys displeasure with a pinkie. Pleases
herself with pearls. Knits one. Purls two.
Knows when to stopper whiskey. Knows when
to whisk the pretty girls away—how they are
fluttering among the men is how trouble flaps
its wings before it lands. Wins games of gin.
Drinks gin from secret thimbles in her purse. Is
pursed. Is buttoned down the center. Centers
the centerpiece so that flowers bloom in
symmetry. Delights in symmetry like knife to
fork, like night to wine uncorked, like cork to
what is open as a mouth. Will not say cock.
Says women are the national bird. Boards up
the house at sideways rain. Reigns queen of
every son belongs to her, the way a wife
belongs inside stone walls. Wills passerines to
drop white feathers for a hat. Hates dropped or
scattered leaves that leave the courtyard in a
disarray. Disdains the wedding sheet unstained.
Disdains new things. Disdains the common
dove that hobbles in a cage, pink and gray—
poor female of the breed—lifting its beak to
make a voice like speaking.

House of the Small Dictatorship

Tripe soup for supper: because a man's belly must be full when he surveys the terrain of the kitchen table.

Look, there's the woman he married and there his daughter's porcelain face.

And before the soup, a glass of limonada to whet the tongue like a knife.

Sometimes he takes his coffee on the terrace. Sometimes he takes his wife.

The radio plays at a fingersnap. The paper opens on its own.

If there are cigars, they clip themselves. They light into an orange tip.

Go cut papaya and bring it here, he says.

And other proclamations: that dogs belong underfoot, that girls to the rule of crinoline.

He tells the guava tree to stop its stench of garbage. He tells the parrot to keep things shut.

And though the fruit keeps stinking, the bird still shits the windowsill, inside the house a tyranny of slippers.

A tyranny of sherbet for dessert.

The Epileptic

Conversations with him are like waiting for thunder. Between the long pauses, she pours herself another cup of tea. If this is marriage, then it's a mystery—those pills he takes for headache, for instance, and when he claims the afternoon is the smell of rotten fruit. Sometimes he sees the air as yellow lines. Objects grow small or very large, depending on his sleep. This has happened before, he says. He says, I've never seen your face before. At parties, everyone waits while he stares into the middle distance of a room, at the vase perhaps, or pink hibiscus blooms. You're a stranger, he says. And she agrees. They lie without touching for weeks. Only later, when she leaves, does she learn the name for this disorder. All the transient signs: the pale halo of secrets around him.

The Woman in the Grocery Store

In one version of the story, she's third person.
And he's attacker who held her for a day. Never
name. Not even last name first, as in official
document, as in report in triplicate. Right now,
she's running through the frozen foods. She
crosses into aisle seventeen. And then she's
point of view where everything stands feet
away, canned beans so close you almost touch
them as you round the corner into cereal and
snacks. And where is no name with the knife?
You know he's waiting by the pyramid of
mayonnaise. Or else, the pillowed stack of
marshmallows in plastic sacks. The bruise is
angry on your face. You, first person now, the
eye that sees the automatic door slide open,
shut again, caught inside the stuttering of
doors. The exit to this place so wide, I think. No,
narrow in its green fluorescent stare.

Still Life

After, you see chipped plaster and know the
mark that knuckles make. Observe the chair on
its side, like a body kicked. A chain dangling
from the front door. This is how to tell a story.
This is how to reconstruct the scene: and here
is where he made her sit, and here is where she
bit the fleshy edge of his hand. They waited
hours here, still life with daisies, spittle of blood.
The room, a dark idea of rooms. And then the
day, a gleaming penknife drawn across the
floor.

Hostage

Nano painting by Frederik de Wilde, 2010

All light is taken hostage in its frame. What it reflects is nothing but itself and, in this way, becomes the blackest room, a square of blackened heat. Inside this place can be the black of someone doing harm. Perhaps, a man creeps in upon a girl—she sleeps within this outer space of black, this hyperblack, this night unperforate. Can darkness be a thing observed if all around is dark? We say blackhearted. We say black magic. We say blackout to mean the terror of the scene.

Domesticated Fowl of the Sula Valley

The birth of consciousness is chickens in the yard. One day they're squawk and feathers, a group of bodies scattering for feed. The next they're boiled dinner on the child's plate. Chicken? she cries as a question, Chicken? Outside the window: other birds designed for disappearing. There is the cockatiel that has a history with words. Missionary? the birdie asks, Or doggie-style? When the child gestures at the empty perch, her parents say How Sad It Flew Away. So many birds go missing. There are shadows the girl flutters with her hands. There is her daddy, his nose so like a beak. The downy voice of her mother is muffled in the sheets.

My Mother Wonders—

that night, if there had been a dog beside her in bed, curled up, its back against her back (as dogs will do), or else spread wide, in sleep made monster-long (unleashed, unfenced), perhaps its muzzle twitching with a bark because it dreamed of other dogs, it gnawed on bones, it nuzzled at the bellied dark and tasted milk—she asks, would it (oh god)

have pawed the man, a shape that smelled like booze and smoke and something else—would it have bit the man who held the knife—or when the bruise was fingers on my mother's face, would it have curled (bad dog) into a tighter band of nose-to-tail? Or licked the (awful) hand?

Lapdog

When he bites her wrist, his teeth leave bracelet indentations. Nothing to terrify or keep her hand away. Always she smoothes the cut velvet of his coat, unknots a mat, unfurls the tassel of his tail. He's footstool. He's wagging metronome. He's throw pillow laid heavy on the couch. Some dogs are built for violence, their jaws like cages that capture what they chew. But he's a jewel box small enough to hold a pair of wedding rings. The only thing he murders is a bone. This is true domesticated bliss. He follows her from room to hungry room as if she's kibble in a plastic pouch, as if she is both water and the bowl. And if we're being honest, she follows him as well: to the front door where night is lifting its own dark snout, the breezes full of squirrel and hollyhock, the shadow-musk of raccoon. He makes small circles of his fear, their bodies so near it's hard to tell which one of them is shivering at the cool, incisive slivers of the moon.

Shot through with Holes

On Upland Terrace, the worst menace was a blue jay that pecked the neighbor's cat. Raccoons knocked over cans. The brave ones climbed our second story, looking in. Bandits, my mother called them. Once, ten blocks away, a man was killed. My mother said, Not far from here and Just the other day. For a year she said that, as if any punctured body was Right Now and Right Outside this house. The summer of cicadas, our magnolia almost died—each leaf shot through with holes. The air was full of insect violins, like a movie where the music lets you know a stranger is just about to stab. That same June, we came home to an open door. My mother stood at the threshold. Was it the wind? Or a latch not catching as it should? I don't remember if she asked me then or later on. We dialed my father from a neighbor's phone. The police shined lights at all our closets, pushed coats aside to check the corners. I don't remember if they sighed or rolled their eyes. Nothing, they said. Ma'am, there's nothing here.

In Honduras, My Grandmother
Dreamed of Germany

Green apples in a season of papaya. Green
apples at the rainy time. No apples. Only warm
tortillas here, each day cast iron that refuses
cold, milk gone sour in the sweating glass.
Here's tamarind, cake from masa, plantains
turned caramel. Is it possible that in another
country she was tweed, and everywhere a
waltz? Here, she wears white gauze. Trees
keep dropping stones, avocados so hard they
make a sound like something knocking shut—
memory a barrel, green scent that rises from
the wood.

Interview

Can you describe the man in question? Can you describe the man? Between the hours of what and what? Between what street and where? Please indicate the places on your body. Can you turn left? Please face the other way. Can you recall his face? Do any of these faces look like his? Look closely at each face. Do any of these names? Name three important features. What other parts of him? Was it a rose? Was it a rose with letters underneath? What kind of ink? All black? Or black with pink? What kind of voice? Could you identify the voice behind the glass? Can we go back? How did he enter when he entered? How did he go? Can we go back to earlier? How did you know the man? Can we go back? Was there a lock? A key? What did he ask? How many times? Please say how many times. Can you describe the man again? How tall he was, how thin? Can you repeat the question that he asked? Can you repeat the question? Can you repeat? Repeat it, please.

Story

The woman is telling a story—how many cigarette burns, that the camps were called HOUSES, the riverstone of her body. My mother asks, How many cigarette burns? and waits for translation: this is the word for RIVER, this is the word for RAVISH. Thank god for translation. And my mother—whose job is to record that RAVISH means to carry off—writes words like SYSTEMATIC. My mother's job: record the sequence of events. First this. Then this. In her reports to Washington, the right word is SYSTEMATIC. She tries to hold the sequence of events in her reports to Washington. First this. Then this. Then later this. Twenty years ago, my mother was telling a story. She tries to hold the memory of that man, his knife, his hands. He could have killed her. Years ago, my mother was telling a story. All of this is water: the memory of that man, his knife, his hands, what he could have killed, each word like a water glass, all of it water—the camps called HOUSES, words glass and breakable. The woman is telling her story.

Dubrovnik

No picture is proof of anything. Even the snapshot from 1981, the one where we are leaning in clean light—even that photograph is real as any view perceived through gauze that is, unreal, implausible. So when my mother says that oysters laid her sick for half a year or that, in general, the body is assailed, all I can think is someone told me I saw Dubrovnik when I was six—the scene from our window clear as a postcard of the Adriatic Sea. And there was a dining room lit by lamps in the shape of sailing ships, each vessel luminous with its journey. All I can think is perhaps I climbed a stairwell carved in stone, ten years before the city was besieged, that Dubrovnik did exist as walls around walls around walls—and that perhaps my mother once stood on a rocky beach, like a beautiful city untouched at the vulnerable points.

Lost Photograph of Trotsky, from the Family Album

In that snapshot of Leon with Great-Uncle
So-and-So they're slouching somewhere
equatorial, two Jews exiled in direct sunlight.
To the right: a cactus, which reminds them it's
thirsty this work—to stand for the workers. To
the left: some sand as if to say Keep Walking.
My mother, who learned to read by reading the
socialist news, recalls the boat she took to
America (the SS *Metapan* of United Fruit Co.),
the air gone sweet with bananas left sitting in
the sun. Passengers tasted pineapple in their
sleep. And docked in New York, everyone hid
red kerchiefs. They forgot the words to "The
Internationale" or dropped them over the side
the way one puts away a photograph, not
because it's worthless but because it's
evidence of somewhere distant, someplace
sepia and blurred.

Portrait of My Mother's First Husband, with Fabergé Objects

I want to say he isn't bad—that every story needs a man who lifts an egg against the light to find the hairline crack. Already his fingers have found a flaw in the enamel, and the clasp that doesn't always catch. If we leave him long enough he'll fumble every heirloom with the clumsiness of affection. How he lingers on beautiful things.

The gems are precious for their cage of prongs and filigree. Inside the rounded box: a bird with fractured wings. And the carriage only moves when someone drags the golden horses by their chains. In this world of jeweled diminutives, he reaches—a giant or a god—from a sky of lapis lazuli to right the palace gone crooked in its case.

The Blue Dress

That day, tired of playing dollies and Let's
Pretend, I found folded silk in the bottom
drawer, pushed to the back behind sheets and
pillowcases, blue silk like skin near drowning,
each button a drooping pearl. There were
albums I pulled from other drawers, faces
behind plastic film, the young couple framed
with black corners. In each photograph, my
mother's face was water just before a stone
drops in, surface-smooth, opaque. That our
parents have lives before us is a secret we
close in a dark compartment, the blue dress a
body dragged from a lake.

Ode to Breaking Things

It should be a fairy tale: the cracked girl, the father who dreams of gilded things, the suitor from a country called savior.

My mother accepts the ring. She takes her gift of coffee beans, whole fields of them, acres for days of the week.

Her wedding comes with a house, the way some weddings come with crystal in a cardboard box. Evenings the courtyard goes pink, the portico a series of arched bones.

At a certain point, she begins to break dishes trimmed with birds of paradise.

This is a poem about captivity.

Big spaces small as smaller ones, windows painted shut, the stone mosaic held inside its own design of roses.

The neon parakeet gives up its cage to the irritation of hands, first the door-hinge torn, then tiny bars, at last the food bowl loses its pinch of seeds.

Soon she considers her husband. Each of his treasures catch the afternoon, ships the length of toothpicks sailing on and on their bottled seas, plaques honoring this Notable and That.

Was married. Is married. May marry again. Notice the lemon tree and the slice of lime in every glass.

Something to do with sourness. For a year, she is Mrs. Someone Else. So beautiful in all those photographs I've never seen.

His pen drinks ink with a thirst she can't stand. Imperative to snap the channel, bend the nib. A must to drop the well.

Two people can be glass on glass.

The only thing to do is grind together into powder. The only thing: become a chance for shards.

Doubt

His hands were paperweights, heavy enough
to hold a woman down. Sit there, he said, Now
speak. Did I believe the story—a man broke in
but stopped from breaking in? Sometimes I did.
Sometimes I saw a picture of a pinioned thing.
A man broke in. Why stop with doors, the
slivering of light? He broke whatever looked like
he could crack. The snap, the tearing sound.
But no, he never did. Instead, the weight of him
was only wrist and ankle. That's what she said.
The truth of it? Perhaps a piece of onionskin, a
carbon copy kept in place.

Eros and Psyche

Sculpture by Antonio Canova, 1787

From a certain vantage point they could be lovers—the man with his arms encircling my mother, and both of them gone marble. He has woken her with the sound of broken wings. Her blanket is polished rock, cold and weighted to the bed. From this angle the knife is hidden, although it's there, the way an arrow is always shooting through this story, desire a dart that finds the tender spot. Bodies make a space for gods to intervene. Tonight if there are souls like butterflies, then they have stilled. If beauty could be bolted in a box, if a deity could say, Don't open this, then my mother might stay asleep forever, unbothered by the monument of those hands.

Willful Abandonment

This is to certify: she has observed the waiting period. She is prepared to file. A bona fide attempt was made to tolerate the way he chews his steak, his choice of green cologne. She made an honest declaration of her allergies, but still he brought her lilies every week. What began as mutual consent became infringement of her closet space. There was gross neglect of the quiet window in her afternoon. This cannot stand. To fulfill her promise would imply a further loss, relinquishing all claim to the dotted dress she wore at seventeen. Conditions of the bond do not include old diaries. She'll pay the fine if ordered. She'll place her hand on a stack of books. She'll swear. The trustee is instructed to keep his box of chocolates. Desist from velvet hearts. Enough with white bouquets. Sometimes a woman leaves so quickly she cannot pack. No defense. She is without a vested ownership in wedding rings, without intent to phone. This is to certify: from time to time, she liked it here. On certain dates, the body gave in to its forgetfulness. She concurs a party may be found at fault—perhaps the china pattern, the silverware, those silver flowers etched into each knife.

Tower

Painting by Roberto Aizenberg, 1950

Think of exile as a city. The tongue is a green
tower.
                    There are regular intervals
of steps, sequence of holes called windows.
Gates keep someone out and someone in.

Think of all the letters home: I write to tell you
that even here there's sky, a horizon painted
white, light a perforation in the east.

Another word for architect is loneliness.

            Rooms avoid meeting in their concrete
symmetry. Each turret stands parallel to the
next.

Linen

I think of my mother's family, circa 1936—
folding Warsaw and Berlin in their steamer
trunks,

beneath prayer shawls, pictures of the dead.
That, shipped to Honduras,

they learned to speak new languages the way
they learned to eat

tortilla after years of bread. That they built
history in walls, shelves for books,

windows framing a street that wasn't Stuttgart
or Odessa. There would be a table for their
meal,

a box of charity. Candles would stop them
getting lost. That all of us need an entrance,

even here, a post on which to pin a prayer, a
door to creak when prophets enter,

or when angels. That all of us carry home like a
steerage ticket crumpled in our hands.

My Mother, Temporarily Disowned

For seven days she was gone to them. They sat in a room the way mourners do, mirrors dressed in black, black garments rent at the sleeves. Daughter: a synonym for disloyalty. In that week after her dying, friends arrived with food under glass. Her name was placed on a silver tray or poured into a pitcher. She became pictures of the dead—Our Little Girl In Blessed Memory. They washed their hands. They washed their hands of her. If she had phoned, her voice would have sounded like a spirit entering the cold body of the earpiece, some dybbuk calling through the twisted cables of grief.

Chronic Pain

At seventeen, I watched my mother dress—
tucked and zipped, skirt sharp as a pencil—
how she paused, pressed fingers to her chest.
No one knew the bruise of her breathing. There
were pills she took for numbness. Pills for sleep.
Pills for being a nerve exposed to air. She was
modern, which meant even on bad days, my
mother climbed a chair to change the blown-
out bulb, perched on a rung until daylight
shuddered on. I liked her best in shoulder pads
or a pair of heels that announced her body's
clattering. On bad days, she held her neck
together with a scarf, pinned a brooch to the
hurt lapel. On bad days—the man who rubbed
a knife across her skin as in some metaphor for
pain. That year I learned from Ibsen a woman
must be bird or suicide, Nora Helmer or Hedda
Gabler. I remember my mother as often lying
down—tender spots and trigger points, a flare-
up when it rained. How small she was beneath
the wool and panty hose. She lay on the orphan
of furniture we called a fainting couch, Victorian
as the old hysteria I read about in Freud—Dora
who dreamed the bed on fire, only her jewel box
saved.

When Her Father Was Losing at Poker, Her Mother Said

Go count the chips at Daddy's elbow—how high or low the stack. Count coins. Count fingers of scotch in the crystal, by which I mean how much liquid in the man. Where is the rabbit foot? The medal pressed with symbols of the fortunate? If daddy puffs cigars, see that he burns no paper. Listen to Daddy laugh. There will be something round in his voice, a zero that is another sound for hungry. As for the folded mouth of his wallet, make sure that it stays shut. If he complains that money talks, tell him that silence is a wife who can fill her jar with jangling. Tell him front doors lock from inside, bed empty as a bankbook. Tell Daddy that luck is a room voided of smoke, all winnings dragged from the felt. Luck is the torn-up promissory note, the crushed aspirin, the brown taste of morning in his throat.

Café con leche

It's ten thirty at night. My mother leans across
the stove to check the boil on the milk, whisk in
her left hand, a jar of Folgers in her right. Her
mouth purses in what looks like a kiss but is
only a little breath to stop the liquid from forming
a skin. We've been standing in the kitchen,
talking about marriage, not wanting to sit or fall
asleep. So she uses the recipe she learned as
a little girl. Sometimes, she says, what's
sweetest and most flavorful comes from the
fake stuff. I watch her dissolve brown crystals in
the pot. It's true. The coffee tastes like coffee.
With my eyes closed, I can't tell the difference,
which has always been the problem for women
in my family—the way so many of us would
rather drink something instant, that bitterness
can be hidden with enough spoonfuls of sugar,
or how good it feels to burn our fingers on a
chipped, ceramic mug.

The Replacement Ring

This time my husband buys one-size-too-small,
the band resisting water, soap, unbudgeable no
matter how he worries it, so that soon he quits
trying to pry it from his hand, the arc carving a
concave pinkness in his skin. The metal looks
shiny beside my ring, a gleaming difference of
years, all those knocks and scratches, which
come from moving objects and ourselves. I can
hardly remember how it felt at first—to put on
the sudden weight of platinum, when salt or
weather seemed to shrink the loop. This, my
husband says, is marriage. Something difficult
to fit. And once we enter it, once we slide inside
its circle, we learn to bend our bodies to its
curve.

Set Jerusalem above My Highest Joy

—Psalm 137

Every marriage is arranged to be broken.
There is the light bulb wrapped in a napkin,
which the groom wedges beneath his heel.
We say mazel tov at the snap of glass. It's
tradition: this ruined temple, this mandatory
grief. The bride is wrapped in cloth. No one
can see her incandescence—we're all too
busy saying luck has happened here. She's
burning with a last electricity that comes from
being wholly all alone. It's hard to hear her
shatter. We stomp our feet to the shudder of
the accordion. It gasps then holds its breath
again.

My Mother Hurts Her Hand Again

We should worry when her thumb is noosed by the dog's extendable leash. We should knock cubes of ice from their plastic beds. We should worry when the kitchen drawer slides shut—A Mind Of Its Own, my mother says. And perhaps she has a point, just as table edges are sure to press the bruised line of her palm, that deep uncertainty where life nearly crosses love, and fate is a vanity that drops its wooden top on the tips of her fingers.

Bethesda

On the front page: homicide. Blunt force trauma. One girl. Another left alive, almost able to speak when she's found on the floor of the upscale yoga store. For a week the story is two men anonymous in their masks. Assailants, the papers say. We place candles near the crime scene, bouquets of flowers, pictures of the dead, as if violence were an altar to which pedestrians might pray. For a week we use words like random. We call the one who lived poor thing. On page four: photos of Bethesda, so familiar in its fancy paper shops and boutique wines that we know a wound can happen anywhere. Even when we learn—in a shocking twist, the papers say—that there were no men, that the murderer was the girl who lived, that she cut and bound herself and lay on the ground, waiting for someone to find her, even then it's hard not to believe in randomness. Something in her snapped, the papers say. The dark is full of knives. And anger is a name we give to the unnamable. Bethesda, house of mercy, house of grace, shallow waters where we wash our hands.

The Leap

Wait Until Dark, 1967

In that moment after Hepburn stabs the man—
Audrey in her pink sweater, her neck a sharp
arrangement made of bone—the room is
almost mute, lighted just enough for us to watch
her feeling—don't leave the stairs, we think—
feeling for escape, and the violins—which turn
everything more terrible—hush for a moment,
hush. Window! she cries and stumbles down
the stairs, over another body lying there. Then
just as she's almost safe, almost reached the
outside world of the window, Alan Arkin is
leaping—catlike, we think—impossibly high
and beautiful, the knife she stabbed him with,
now clawing air, and the strings have started up
again, as if to say, dear ones, this, this is the
voice of fear.

What I Saw in the Water; Or, What the Water Gave Me

Painting by Frida Kahlo, 1938

Those could be my mother's toes in the bathtub,
red-nailed for the things they've rubbed against.
Only her feet and legs. As is the way with
parents, how we see parts of them, the rest
beyond frame. Assume she has a body. Assume
that buildings burn inside of her. That, like Frida,
names can change. Like weather, like national
costume. The white dress is designed for
pleasing men. Hibiscus folds the petals of itself,
and here a skeleton. Here, birds and women on
their backs. In the painting oil is oil-on-water. In
the painting's populated dream—family is a
thing that hurts the spine. Family a self-portrait,
naïve retablo on a square of a tin.

Family Business

The seamstress proves her skill by becoming invisible. A red thread hides itself inside a hem. A sock gives up its hole. Chain stitch and featherstitch. Lock and overlock. Tailor's tack. My mother sews each afternoon beside her mother, bribed by-the-inch to baste: a peppermint for a seam, a pair of caramels for a collar. Sometimes it's dresses need taking in. Sometimes a button X-ed in place. Sometimes—no, always—she hates the sound of scissors dragged through cloth. Cross-stitch. Topstitch. Whip. Catch. My mother hates the No. 12 needle, the small rut it makes in her finger. In another room her father plays at cards. You are a small and weak person, he often says. Backstitch. Blind stitch. Blanket. The women in my family are broderie anglaise, surface of cutwork and lace, so easily torn, so devoted to ornament.

Garment Industry

Q: What's the difference between a tailor and a
poet?
A: One generation.

—Yiddish joke

My mother lifts a seam ripper, its miniature
hook made for a world of tiny violence.

Not only for ripping seams, she says.

There is a thread between us: we work at a
humming machine.

We are shirtwaist and sonnet.

She splits body from sleeve, neck from yoke.

I sift through rag paper, write down the
sound of tearing fabric.

Look. Look at the dress we sew from the shreds
of other things.

Strawberry Thief

Furnishing textile, William Morris (1883)

That the Victorians hate emptiness is plain from
the doubling of wings, clusters of flowers,
berries bunched

in twos and threes—open space frightening as
an orchard after dark. The night is dyed indigo
(on pillows,

cotton drapes), fruit tinted madder red, bleach
sharpening the border. But beyond the printed
cloth,

now displayed at the Victoria & Albert Museum,
hangs the real story—a kitchen garden
unguarded,

Morris watching as birds strip sweetness from
the stems. After, the only virtue is adornment of
the plot—

that the artist can draw berries back on the
naked patch, what little emptiness held by
yellow beaks.

Met Parents My How

—before New York City and City Hall—before
a mutual friend arranged it all—Sidney or was
it Sydney—before my mother ran away—there
were tea tiny cakes on porcelain—bowls of
aspic—a parrot talking secrets to its perch—
before she married an earlier man—Richard or
sometimes Ricardo—before El Salvador—
before she was made to marry—her father
said—the money—so good this would be for
family—before the man inside the room could
stop other men from entering—his weight a
stone—before bruises—or long before who
knows about chronology—my father ended
things by mail—the envelope stamped red—
she was crying before—the cut on her head—
the bruises—before the handyman broke in—
my mother slept alone—before Gauloises—
before Pernod—my father left for Paris—before
kisses in the green backseat of cars—before
the heat of everything—when he answered
Nice to meet you—and she—before Hello—
before My Name's Jeannette—began—

Schiller

Everything that is hidden, everything full of
mystery, contributes to what is terrifying and is
therefore capable of sublimity.

—"On the Sublime"

The man with the knife is capable of sublimity.
The man with the knife is capable. The man is
capable of holding her in place. He holds her in
a place called home. In a place called home, a
man with a knife. In a place called knife, a man.
In a place called man, a knife that splits the
home from home. And later, it won't be a home
to her. Will only be the knife, the man who holds
the knife, the knife again. Always the knife again
and the hand that holds the knife. In a place
called knife, she's there, mistaking knife for
night, and night for mystery. Everything a
mistake. The shadow-body of a man can hold a
knife. The shadow made by words can hold the
knife, not very long, away from her. Away from
her, the hand. The capable hand. The man in
his sublimity. Away, the home no longer home.

Light Switch

Chairs are made visible as chairs. Books aren't obstacles but bent, flipped open, or standing up. Bound. The lighted room is like the scary man unmasked, when credits roll and everyone rises from the ache of seats, brushing popcorn from laps. There's nothing frightening here. And though the light switch is only spring and terminal, quick-break, the small push of contact, there's still some kind of magic in its copper spark. So we reach around the door, touch the plastic toggle the way the pious touch a prayer scroll. The bulb blinks on. Shadows are shoved back into corners. And we enter this room, or any room, walk forward into the incandescent certainty that there are no surprises. Nothing is crouched and waiting with a knife.

Notes

"Arranged Marriage, as Coffee Field"—Ellen Bryant Voigt's "Winter Field" serves as both starting point and conversation.

"Hostage"—Much of the poem's information about "Nano art" comes from the website of artist Frederik de Wilde.

"Shot through with Holes"—The title comes from an essay about memory and trauma, by Henri Raczymow.

"Café con leche"—This poem is modeled on Tony Hoagland's "Windchime."

"Bethesda"—The Pool of Bethesda, which is in the Muslim Quarter of Jerusalem, appears in the Gospel of John, as a site of miraculous healing.

"Light Switch"—This poem is built on the scaffolding of Bob Hicok's "Alzheimer's."